DAVID WILLS

PRODUCT RESEARCH 101

**The Essential Guide on How to Find the Perfect Niche and
Product That Sells, Discover How to Find Hot Niche
Markets and Winning Products That Would Sell**

Descrierea CIP a Bibliotecii Naționale a României
DAVID WILLS
   PRODUCT RESEARCH 101. The Essential Guide on How to Find the Perfect Niche and Product That Sells, Discover How to Find Hot Niche Markets and Winning Products That Would Sell / David Wills. – Bucharest: Editura My Ebook, 2020
   ISBN

DAVID WILLS

PRODUCT RESEARCH 101

The Essential Guide on How to Find the Perfect Niche and Product That Sells, Discover How to Find Hot Niche Markets and Winning Products That Would Sell

My Ebook Publishing House
Bucharest, 2020

TABLE OF CONTENTS

INTRODUCTION

The one thing everyone seems to want these days is to start their own business. Many new business owners believe that the only thing they need to be successful is a website that will bring in automated profits around the clock.

While a site is a useful tool to have, it isn't a full-fledged business. Unfortunately, many would-be entrepreneurs are not prepared to put in the effort that is required to research a niche correctly to determine that the niche they want to work in is a paying one.

Finding a paying niche, and then creating content, products, and services for that niche, is the best way to for you to build a solid foundation for a successful online business. It is also the best way to achieve the level of success and kind of profits that most business owners need to make their efforts worthwhile.

Not picking a lucrative niche is an easy mistake to make when you are excited about all the great ideas that you have. It is also easy to fall into a niche that you've heard people are making a killing selling online.

Passion and enthusiasm are essential when it comes to running your own business, but so is research. All the large corporations spend time researching before releasing new products to the public to see if there is any interest in a new product.

Unfortunately, most new business owners get it wrong. They first create a product, then spend the time and money to launch the product, then try to mind a market for it.

The secret key to online success is to:

- Find a paying market

- Create a product for it

- Launch the product by directly marketing to the paying market you've already located.

The best niche marketing strategies and tactics are based on concrete research and building a relationship with the prospective customers in your niche.

While there is a lot of popular niches out there, not all of them are paying, or even well-paying ones. While you can make money with 'bargain basement' kinds of customers, it is much better if you create products for people who are willing to pay a reasonable price for real solutions to the issues they are facing.

This is the basis for a sustainable business, with happy, loyal customers that will come back regularly to buy from you. In fact, if you do things right, some of your customers will be so loyal that every time you launch a new product, they'll be willing to buy it.

Without doing the proper research, you may end up putting in hours of time and effort only to discover that you don't have a real viable business after all. Your attempt to get your blog or website set up and to try and create a product to sell will be a waste of time unless you know your niche is part of a paying market.

Once you are sure you have chosen the right niche in a paying market, you will start to earn the profits you need to meet your financial goals.

CHAPTER 1

WHY FINDING YOUR NICHE IS IMPORTANT

A niche is a small, specific, target market of potential customers. Smart business owners try to sell their products and services to a niche base of customers by conducting detailed market research with a focus on trying to understand the consumer behavior of the people who are interested in that niche. Specifically, their needs, concerns, and desires.

Once the research shows that consumers that are interested in the niche are willing to pay for products, services, and solutions that are related to the niche, the business will then try to cater to them as much as possible by providing a range of items for sale at various price points.

Some of the products they offer will have a much broader appeal than others. For example, there will be more customers interested in golf products for beginners, than those looking for advanced information on golf because they are or are hoping to become a pro golfer.

Therefore, by focusing on products for beginners, you will be able to increase sales based on volume by offering a lower price point to a more significant amount of customers.

However, while there may be fewer advanced students looking for information and products on golf, the exclusive, high-level information that you can provide could command a much higher price than the eBooks focusing on a beginner's level.

Offering advanced students, a course, multimedia package, coaching program, membership program, or other similar products could command a much higher price point, especially if you are seen as an expert in your niche.

This is because the more credentials you have, the more money you can charge for the products and services you are offering in your niche, within reason.

Your price point has to be within reason because finding the right niche isn't just about finding the right one that pays, but it is also about what people are buying and how much they are willing to pay for them.

If the average price they are willing to pay is $29.95 and you want to enter the market with a $39 product, there will need to be an apparent reason why your product is worth more.

Your expertise, credentials, and the added extras you are offering can help to remove some of the doubt in the customer's mind and convince them that the extra cost is worth it. However, you will only be able to convince them to pay the extra money if you know what other offers are available so that you can make an even better offer.

As you research your niche, you will not only discover if it is a paying one but if there are users who are willing to pay premium prices for the kind of insider information that you can provide.

You also want to think about the life cycle of the customer in a niche. While they might start out as a beginner, by sticking with the niche and continuing to learn, they will eventually need to obtain intermediate or advanced information.

Understanding the life cycle of your customers provides you with the opportunity to continue to sell to them over and over again.

In niche marketing, the general rule is that 80 percent of your profits will come from 20 percent of your customers. There are specific niches where it might actually by 90/10.

When you take care of your existing customers, they will continue to buy from you on a regular basis every time you have a new product or service to offer them that will meet their needs.

You can earn income around the clock by automating a process with a range of offers pre-loaded in an email marketing platform. This can then be delivered to your prospects on a regular basis.

You can create your product, set up your order flow, write your sales letter, point traffic to it, and watch your visitors turn into paying customers on your email marketing list.

With niche markets, you can have a single product that will automatically sell for weeks, months or even years to come. Once you have created a successful product, all you have to do is continue to drive traffic to your sales page.

Creating a good sales letter will help convert visitors into customers at least one to five percent of the time. That means that for every 100 visitors to your site, one to five people will buy your product.

Every niche is different regarding needs, acceptable price points, and consumer behavior. This is why it is so important to do your research long before you enter the market.

This will allow you to know if a niche will be profitable or not before you waste your time, money, and energy. This provides you with the opportunity to set realistic goals and expectations as you launch your business.

As you research your niche business, you will need to determine who your ideal customer is, what their needs are, where you can find them, if they are willing to pay for the items you feel they need, and how much they'll pay for those products and services.

Through market research, you can determine how much your niche customers will be willing to pay for similar products.

CHAPTER 2

CHOOSING YOUR NICHE

As you begin your journey into starting your own niche marketing business, you want to start by jotting down your ideas for a niche that you would like to work in and the reasons behind your interest.

There are many reasons for working in a niche. Many people decide on their niche because it's a hot and trending market. While it's okay if you want to jump on the bandwagon of new and emerging markets, you have to be prepared to be nimble and put in the hard work to stay ahead of the curve.

However, some trends can be quick moving, while others aren't that interesting or exciting, or sustainable. Significant events like the Olympics or the presidential election can generate a ton of buzz and demand for memorabilia, but it will quickly drop off as soon as the event is over.

These kinds of niche markets will only allow you to be in business for a short period before you have to find another niche that will be profitable.

Niches that don't expire too soon, or at all, are referred to as 'evergreen.' An evergreen niche may not have as much excitement as the latest gadget, but they are more stable and can keep your business running for years.

Being evergreen means that the products and services that you are selling should be able to keep you earning a profit year after year. You also should try to find a niche that is interesting enough to make it fun and enjoyable for you to go to work every day.

For many, choosing a niche is easy because they base their business on their own personal interests and expertise. Be an expert in what people are looking for in that niche can be a good thing.

It will give you a pretty good idea as to whether or not the niche will be profitable, to begin with. In other words, if you buy products in the niche, chances are there are other people out there that will buy them as well.

However, it is essential for you to keep in mind that people won't always behave in the manner that you expect. While you may think that your idea is a terrific one, without doing the proper niche research, it could bomb, leaving you with the realization that there is no paying market for it after all.

A common mistake that you'll want to try to avoid is spending your time creating a product, website, and more, for a niche that is worth little or nothing because it is not a paying market, or because you're targeting the wrong audience.

You need to listen to what people are saying, and figure out what problems and challenges they have, then offer a solution to those challenges. By conducting research and getting to know your prospective customers better, you can find out what actions they are willing to take to achieve their goals.

Doing in-depth analysis before you start working on your product will save you months of hard work for zero profit.

Selling as an Affiliate

Marketing as an affiliate is the easiest way to make money when you first start your business. Becoming an affiliate of top companies like Amazon gives you access to millions of products that you already know are in demand.

Depending on the reward system you choose and the products you are selling in specific niches, you can start earning commissions as high as 15 percent.

Many of the top companies like Amazon and eBay have their own affiliate programs that are administered in-house. Other companies run their affiliate programs through a marketplace that operates the program for them.

While the most lucrative way to make a profit in your niche is to create your own products and services to sell, there are several reasons why you may want to consider starting out with affiliate marketing.

First and foremost, affiliate marketing is a way to become profitable soon after starting your business. Affiliate marketing also takes less time and energy to get started. The products that you can sell through an affiliate program are a good indicator that the niche is a paying one.

Affiliate marketplaces can also be a valuable place to conduct your research. They allow you to see exactly what people are buying and how much they are willing to pay for the products.

This will give you a good idea of how your own products and services will fit into the paying marketplace. Staring out with affiliate marketing can help you to avoid some of the common mistakes in niche marketing, like setting a price point that is too high or too low or creating products that no one wants.

By doing this research, you'll also be able to see the gaps in your offerings. Therefore, when you are ready to develop your own product or service, your final decision will be based on the research you've conducted because you will have discovered a real need on the part of your prospective clients.

Another reason you may want to consider affiliate marketing is that you can learn a great deal about marketing.

The affiliate marketing programs are usually run by a manager who is an expert in coming up with exciting offers, ideas, and graphics for their offers. Often, they will provide the affiliate marketers with useful tips and hints that can help them sell their products.

To gain a better understanding of how to market your own products, read the emails they send you and take action as suggested. Carefully look at the creative items that they come up with.

Read the sales letters to see how they are constructed. Taking these actions can help to provide you with a crash course in marketing, even if you've never sold anything before.

You can also get suggestions, useful tools, and free material to include in your newsletter, Facebook pages, and more. With the more popular products, and during particular times of the year, they will also send you exclusive flash sales or seasonal offers.

Copy and paste these codes and put them in your emails, on your website or blog, as the signature file in your comments on a discussion forum. Doing this can lead to you soon outselling even experiences affiliates because you are taking the time to keep up with the latest trends and what's hot.

Finally, the more streams of income you have in your business, the more they can create a profit. Your commission checks may not be much to start with each month but increasing your income will be up to you and how many products you can promote.

Getting Started with Niche Research

An important step is discovering your niche market is to identify the keywords that are used by your target market. You need to determine what keywords they are typing in and use them to search the topics and products that are related to your market.

The searches that you uncover will help you know the pain points of the niche customers and what problems they need to solve.

This will help you earn enough profit by grabbing the maximum number of specifically targeted customers that are looking for products and services that are directly related to your niche.

You can use Google AdWords Keyword Tool (https://adwords.google.com/home/tools/keyword-planner/#?modal_active=none) to search out specific words and phrases that are related to your niche market.

The tool is free to use and provides you with the opportunity to find all the relevant keywords that are being used by your target customer. You can use the data you gather from this tool to research the specific products, services, and solutions in a niche market and figure out which ones apply to your particular area of expertise.

Once you've identified some of the keywords and phrases that are associated with your niche, you can begin to identify those keywords that have the most profit potential.

You can measure profit potential in three ways:

- High Search Volume

- Low Competition

- Low Cost/Effort to Rank High

Most people try to make an educated guess on those three points, but in the following section, you'll learn how to use the real-world information to eliminate the guesswork.

Finding Hot Keywords

Using Google Keyword Planner, you can estimate the amount of potential visitor traffic, which keywords people are using, and any associated keywords that give you clues as to customers' other requirements.

Your research needs to be focused and in-depth. You need to test as many keywords as is practical until you think that you've covered every keyword or key phrase that a potential customer would use to search for your product or service.

The first piece of data that you will need to look at is if there is a sufficient monthly volume of potential customers actively searching for the product or service you are looking to sell online.

You'll also want to determine if other businesses are already making money from similar products or services. You can do this with Google AdWords Keyword Planner along with search engines like Google, Bing, and Ask.

Organize Your Keywords

Next, you'll want to organize your keywords and key phrases into groups. You can do this by breaking all your keywords down into groups of specific keywords and phrases.

For example, the keyword phrase, "digital camera," can be separated into "underwater digital camera," "underwater digital cameras," and "digital underwater camera." These would be placed in one group while, "digital camera case," can be separated into "underwater digital camera case," and "digital camera cases," and can be placed in another group.

You want to divide separate keywords into groups of no less than 2,000 searches per month. The purpose of doing this is to find a prevailing mindset of groups of people that are looking for similar products, services, information, benefits or features.

To drill down further and discover more potential buyers, you can select the top ten keywords. From these ten keywords, the goal is to try and find a total of 100,000 or more searches in total per month. Every one of these can be added to the Google

Keyword Planner Tool to uncover even more specific long tail keywords.

Now you want to start looking for "Money Making Words" within your list. These buyer keywords signal that people will pay for information. These keywords include, model numbers, brand names, color, buy, cheap, for sale, seller, supplier, etc. The more specific the search, the more likely the customers are to buy.

Next, you can put them in an Excel spreadsheet to find the total number of searches for the top ten keywords. If the number is less than 10,000, it isn't a good market to enter.

Keywords that have a monthly search total of more than 10,000 searches show an okay market, those with 30,000 searches mean it's a good market, and over 100,000 searches per month are the best possible scenario you can have.

Testing Your Keywords Live

The most reliable and inexpensive ways that you can check the potential profit of your keywords is to test them live online. You can upload some keyword specific content to a page on your current blog or website, Facebook fan page, YouTube channel, Pinterest, etc. You can test each piece of new material and see where it lands on Google and how much traffic it brings.

This strategy will allow you to find keywords that have started bringing you traffic organically, that are converting the traffic to revenue, and those that can rank higher. The more traffic the keyword has when ranking lower, the more profit potential it has.

Micro Niches

Remember, if you choose to enter into a popular market, you don't have to start out competing for top keywords. You can compete for less competitive, long-tail keywords instead.

Choosing a micro-niche can become your backdoor entry into the larger niche market.

Once you've decided on the niche market that you want to enter and you've chosen a few keywords, and key phrases, the next step in the process is finding your ideal customer.

CHAPTER 3

FINDING YOUR IDEAL CUSTOMER

Your ideal customer is one who is willing to pay for the solution to their problem. Therefore, you can find your perfect customer by going where they go and offering helpful advice and solutions to their problems. Again, you are looking for a well-stocked pond of hungry, paying customers.

You will be able to offer the solutions in several ways, such as creating free content that will encourage them to view you as an expert and therefore willing to buy your paid content. The one thing that you don't want to do is treat your free content dismissively.

You should look at it like the free samples you get when walking through the supermarket. One taste will hopefully convince people to buy a whole package.

The whole package might transform the initial purchase into the beginning of a long relationship between a new, now loyal customer who becomes a repeat buyer of your brand. If they can't keep buying the same product repeatedly, perhaps they will be willing to try more of your products as they become available.

Always providing your customers what they need and knowing them well you can seem as though you can anticipate their needs. This creates the kind of ideal customer who will sustain your business month after month, year after year.

The more loyal repeat customers you can gain, the more income you will receive on an ongoing basis, and not have too many lean months, but a reasonably predictable, steady income.

You can build your email marketing list by offering them a free newsletter, download, or both, that will allow you to market products and services of interest on a regular basis.

Many of your customers, because they trust your expertise, will buy what you recommend and what you produce, often just because it's you who is recommending or providing the product.

This is the kind of ideal customer that you need to locate or create through high-quality interactions with them in where you can come to be seen as the expert in your niche.

Research and Survey Your Target Market

Once you've identified a profitable niche, you now need to focus on pinpointing precisely what is the audience's pain points. In other words, you need to determine your target audience' most urgent critical problem. Being able to identify the issues your niche is experiencing can be the key to profitability if you can provide them with the best solution.

To identify a need in any niche, you can start by looking at the problems in your own life. Think about what would improve your life, or what would take away one of your life's challenges. You can generally find these answers on popular blogs or niche forums.

Yahoo Answers (http://answers.yahoo.com) is an excellent resource for finding out what solutions to problems people are searching for. Try using the search terms, "help with," "advice on," cure for," followed by your specific keyword.

The solution to your niche audience's problem will be where the most profits lie, whether it's a physical product, a digital product, a service, or information.

You can also start your search with Google Correlate (https://google.com/trends/correlate/). Google Correlate is a tool on Google Trends that enables you to find queries with a similar pattern to a target data series.

The target can either be a real-world trend that you provide or a question that you enter. It uses web search activity data to find queries with a similar pattern to a target data series. The results can then be viewed on the website or downloaded as a .CSV file for you to further analyze.

Creating Your Ideal Customer Profile

After deciding on your niche, you can spend time researching your ideal buyer and defining your target customer's problems, wants, demographics, and then segment them into buyer groups. To help you narrow this down, ask the following questions.

- Where does your target audiences hang out online?
- How active are they online?
- What is their average age and income?
- What motivates them to buy something?
- Are they looking for solutions?

- What do they do?

- What do they consume online?

To get the demographic information on the places they hang out, you can use Quantcast (https://quantcast.com). Quantcast is the world's largest AI-driven audience behavior platform that was designed to understand, influence, convert, and measure the consumer journey, to help marketers discover new customers, drive incremental growth and deliver business outcomes.

Utilize Online Surveys

With the help of several online resources like Survey Monkey (https://surveymonkey.com), SurveyGizmo (https://surveygizmo.com), and Google AdWords, you can utilize online surveys to questions your target audience as to precisely what they want.

The stronger the demand and desire for your product or services, the more probable people are to participate in the survey. You can use incentives like discounts, free downloadable products, or online services the users expected to find when they clicked on your advertisement.

You want to aim for 1,000 responses to your online survey. From this cross-section of your market, you should be able to calculate if enough people are participating in the study to suggest an affordable response rate.

From the information provided in the online surveys you should aim to provide the prospects with (a) precisely what they are looking for, (b) just the way they'd like it, and (c) at the price they are prepared to buy it for. The answers that are given will also provide you with the language you need to use to write your sales copy.

You want to be sure to ask questions about the problems that they are experienced, how difficult it is to find solutions to their problems, what keywords they used to search for solutions, etc.

You can ask for socio/economic/demographic information as well, like age, education level, job, etc. You can even ask them how much they'd pay for a solution and how they'd like it delivered.

There is a qualitative difference between market intelligence, like that, gathered from a survey, and keyword intelligence. Market intelligence can be much more valuable because it allows accurate and confident decision-making regarding marketing and strategic decisions.

The time you spend researching your niche and the ideal customer will be time well spent because it will provide you more than enough ideas on products to create, provided that you have found an eager niche willing to pay for solutions to their problems.

CHAPTER 4

RELATIONSHIP BUILDING IN YOUR NICHE

Once you've determined that you've chosen a paying market, it is time to think about relationship building. To start, you want to locate the main sites, blogs, discussion boards, and forums that are associated with your niche.

Look through each of these to see what topics concerning the niche they are continually discussing. Write down the five most popular issues that are being discussed. This will give you a start on ideas for content on your blog, your newsletter, and possibly a free special report that your potential customers might be interested in receiving for providing you with their email address.

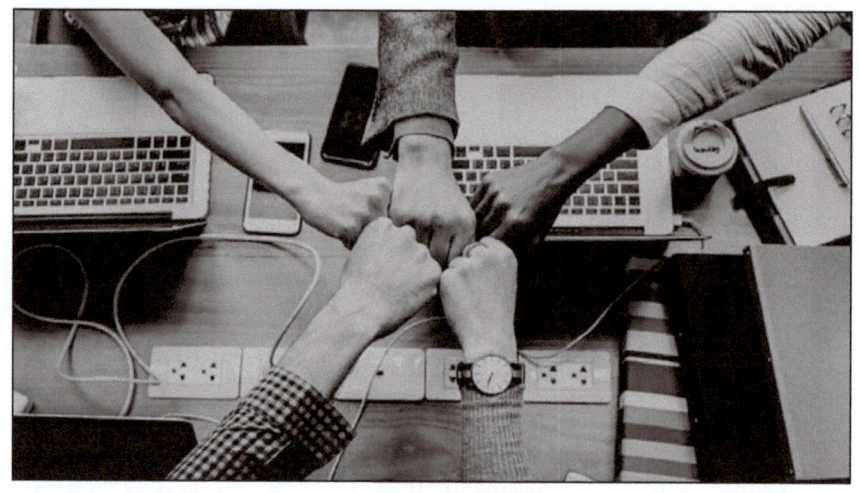

In other words, they are asking to hear more from you, and your email marketing platform can email lists that you will be gathering that can help create a closer connection with potential customers through more regular communication about items of importance.

Posting regularly at social sites will keep your followers updated and make it easier for them to pass along the information to anyone they know who might be interested in it. Always ask for shares and re-tweets and train your target audience to take the actions you wish them to take when you want them to take them.

One of the main reasons you want to start an online business is to make money. However, if this is your only motivation, chances are it will show. Think about a pushy salesperson in a store. You may be polite to them but are usually turned off by their aggressive approach and instantly resist any idea of buying from them.

You probably even try to make a discreet exit as quickly as you can. Others might just walk out as soon as they are confronted.

People online don't have to act politely. They can click out of your page and site, and you will never see them again, and you will be none the wiser as to why they left.

Being able to register them for an e-course or newsletter will provide you a better chance of communicating with them on a regular basis, for building a relationship with them, and building your business brand.

Studies show that it takes at least 17 exposures to a brand or business for people to begin to recognize it and understand what it does and what it represents. Unfortunately, an online business, usually never gets a second chance to make a first good impression.

Email Marketing

Your email marketing campaigns are a valuable resource that provides you with a lifeline of communication with those who are interested in your niche. Give them different reasons to opt-in, such as special reports and newsletters.

If they buy an item, put them on a new customer list, rather than leaving them on a prospects list. You need to treat this list like a precious, rare, and valuable goldmine.

Once you get them on a list, keeping them there can prove to be a challenge. For example, the subscriber may unregister from your list as soon as they obtain the free special report.

This is why an e-course that contains several lessons spaced out over the course of several days and delivered through an autoresponder is a good idea if you want to keep the lines of communication open.

If they do happen to unsubscribe, don't take it personally, but do see if they give a reason. Some people will take the time to tell you. They may feel like they received too many emails, or they don't have enough time, or they decide they aren't interested in any of your offers.

Others will leave and never let you know if you have offended them in some way. You never know what the tipping point will be for a customer in a particular niche.

Sometimes you will have customers on your list for a year or more before they purchase something. Once they do, they may end up buying other items soon after. There might have been some triggering event in their personal life that would have caused them to take action suddenly.

It could have been a purchase for a loved one. It might also have been that after enough communications, they felt more confident that the information was reliable and trustworthy since they saw the quality of the free emails over that period.

Whatever the reason, apparently it can take some time to build a relationship with individual customers.

As a general rule, you can often catch them when they are at their most enthusiastic when they are first coming to your email list. For instance, you can thank them for registering for your free newsletter, and as a special welcome, give them a members-only price to your most popular product at 50 percent off.

If they take the offer, you can then offer them a second product at the special discount of 25 percent off. In this way, you will not only be building a relationship with them by creating the perception that they will save money by staying on the list, but also that you value them as a customer.

Always give your best prices to your best customers, to keep them loyal and see the benefits of being a member. Encourage them to pass along your email to others so they too can get the great deals.

They will probably forward your outstanding offers to others, but that's okay. Word of mouth marketing can quickly spread to a vast number of people.

Your Social Media Accounts

Your social media accounts can also help with this. People on Facebook can like, comment, and share your information. This means that all of the people they are connected to can see your postings too.

This is also a powerful marketing and relationship-building opportunity that can bring in free traffic and sales.

Your product offerings should be varied, with you tracking and testing to see which are the most popular. In this way, you can deliver exactly what they want, at a price they like.

Bundling special price offers can be a powerful tool that can help you increase the dollar amount per customer, per purchase.

Your Newsletter

Your newsletter is your chance to send your customers exciting content on a regular basis that is related to your niche. You can review common issues in FAQs, quizzes, and more.

You can use all the information you've gathered from the forums and discussion boards to provide them with answers to the problems you know they are experiencing.

In this way, you are building relationships and positioning yourself as an expert in your niche without resorting to any aggressive selling. You are providing them offers you are reasonably sure a niche shopper in a paying market will be interested in taking advantage of.

You can choose to email the offers separately, on particular promotional days, or placed within the information email or newsletter. You have to be careful because they may want to opt- out if they get too many overtly commercial emails.

It is all about your customers' wants and needs concerning the niche and how you can build a relationship with them and show them how you can meet those needs. It is about staying on topic in the niche and giving them a range of options related to that niche.

CHAPTER 5

ANALYZING YOUR COMPETITION

Analyzing your competition is essential. Almost every successful business has competition, either direct or indirect. Some competitors are ruthless, so be very careful about examining the competitors in your chosen industry sector before entering it.

While it is true that you need to be aware of your competition, there is no need to feel intimidated by them.

Finding How Many Competitors There Are

The first step in analyzing your competition is to determine how many competitors you have. To do this, you can use Google Search to calculate which websites are targeting the same keywords as you.

If they're using the same keywords in their web page's URL, title, and anchor text, then you know they're serious competition. You can also use Google Search with your chosen key phrase in "quotes" to find out how many competing web pages there are.

You can also find out the number of backlinks to any website with resources like SEOmoz (https://moz.com), Blekko (https://blekko.com), or Majestic Site Explorer (https://majestic.com).

If you want to verify that a website is optimized for your keywords, you can use Google Search to uncover which web pages do have keywords in their page titles, anchor text links, or URL.

Imagine that you want to sell digital camera online, and you want to find out how much quality competition you'll have in themarket.

First, you can find out how many sites have "digital cameras" in the title of their web pages by typing "allintitle:digital cameras" into Google Search. You can also type "intitle:" for each of the keywords you've chosen. You want to avoid competing with websites that have more than 50 relevant keyword backlinks.

Your biggest competitors will be those who are at the top of the search engines for the top three most competitive keywords in your niche.

Researching the Competition

How difficult it will be to rank above your competitors will largely depend on the Page Rank (PR) of their websites and relevant web pages. If the average page rank of the top ten sites is below PR3, then it should take under three months to rank for this keyword.

Using SEO Quake (https://seoquake.com), note the average PR of the top ten websites for each keyword.

To analyze your competitors PR, you can make a spreadsheet, dividing it into two sheets; "Preliminary" and "Market Competition." Put the top ten keywords in the "Preliminary" sheet. On the "Market Competition" sheet, create ten columns; "Site1 PR," "Site2 PR," "Site3 PR," etc. up to "Site10 PR."

Take the best three to five unique search terms and put them in the "Market Competition" sheet.

Next, search Google using the top three keywords. Note the PR of the top ten websites for each of the three to five keywords. You should have 30 in total. Remove the highest and lowest "outliers" and then calculate the average PR in each row and overall.

You may also want to analyze the backlinks of your top competitors to see if they are optimizing their links for the same keywords as you are using.

You can determine the competitiveness of niche keywords by using a tool like Market Samurai (http://www.marketsamurai.com/) or Traffic Travis (https://traffictravis.com). After you've conducted as many searches as necessary, make a shortlist of all the keywords for which you think you can rank highly.

Evaluating the Competition

When you feel like you've found a niche to test and you know the niche's subject matter well enough, you can create a short article, report, e-book, or white paper that offers some vital piece of information about the benefits of your new business idea, product, or service without compromising any of your intellectual property.

You can use this information as the "bait" to acquire a response from your target prospects.

For the last twenty years, internet marketers have proven that people respond best to "ethical bribes." In other words, to get a potential customer's email address or personal details you have to offer them something in return.

That's why publishers of information products like to provide free giveaways in return for opt-in email subscriptions.

Fortunately, larger online brands have not picked up on this tactic yet. Therefore, for you to compete, it is highly recommended you use this strategy.

Look at the biggest brands in the niche you're researching and see how they have evolved. You can find out how long they've been in business under their present domain name by visiting the "Whois" page of Network Solutions (https://networksolutions.com/whois) and find out how long ago the domain name was registered.

Then, using Time Machine (www.timemachine.com) or WayBack Machine (http://archive.org/web/web.php) to see how they have evolved, what they tried that didn't work, and what they kept and where they invested their resources.

You also might want to see which competitors advertise using Pay-Per-Click advertising. If they've been using this form of advertising for a long time, then they are clearly making money.

If it's a niche where the cost of advertising is high, then you can assume that they are making a good profit if they are still in business.

Consider Your Competition's Pricing

If you uncover serious competition during your analysis, subscribe to their email list and see what they're doing. Are they selling higher priced products and services? Alternatively, is it all discounted?

If you uncover some higher prices, then you know that there is a market. If they've continued to offer high priced goods over the years, then you know for sure that the market is sustainable.

If the average price for a product in this niche provides a reasonable profit margin, then it will allow smaller players to enter the market and co-exist with established brands.

However, if the market competes on price, and the margins have been squeezed until they are paper thin, then you're better off looking into a less competitive, more profitable niche.

Also, if everyone is discounting each other in a tiny market, then you'll struggle to get off the ground. However, if there are several tiers of pricing, it's a lot easier for you to not just get into the niche, but to slowly power your way up the pricing levels as well, if you choose.

When it comes to search engine competition, generally, the lower number of competitors the better, However, if you come across a niche that has no competition, you should be suspicious that this could be a niche that no one has been able to make money.

CONCLUSION

A standard medium to success for many small businesses is associating themselves with a niche market. There isn't a single business or entrepreneur that can be all things to its consumers.

There will always be cracks in the consumer populace, whose demands for specific products and services aren't dealt with, giving you the opportunity to supply those unmet demands.

A small business like yours can benefit from these needs that are left unaddressed. The issue is how you can find the right niche market that will help your small business grow. Having a unique or exceptional product will ensure you less competition.

Researching a niche to determine if it has potential requires patience, effort, concentration, the right set of tools, and the ability to ask the right questions and understand the answers you receive.

Take the time to do the research, and it will pay off for you regarding profits. If you chose not to thoroughly research potential niche markets, you would do nothing more than stumble around to try and find the buried treasure that other Internet marketers tell you is out there, but which always seem to evade you.

9 786069 836514

Printed by Libri Plureos GmbH in Hamburg, Germany